JOHN DINNEEN

SUPER-CHALLENGE 2

CONTENTS

Illustrations:
Scoular Anderson

Angus&Robertson
An imprint of HarperCollins*Publishers*

Lemon Teaser

Try this teaser of a challenge and you could become a Lemon Teaser Tamer.

You will need:
A bowl of water.
A lemon.
A coin.

LEMON TEASER

1.
Float the lemon in the water and wait for it to stop moving.

2.
Now carefully balance the coin on the lemon.

How long can you balance the coin on the lemon before it rolls off into the water?

*Very Good - 3 seconds
Lemon Teaser Tamer
- 5 seconds or more*

Nosy Spooner

Hang a spoon on the end of your nose and take the Super Nosy Spooner Award.

You will need:
A teaspoon.

NOSY SPOONER

1.
Put the bowl of the teaspoon over the end of your nose. If you let go of the teaspoon it should hang on the end of your nose. It must not touch your chin or anything except your nose.

2.
If you find it difficult it might help to moisten the end of your nose or find a different shaped teaspoon.

For how long can you hang the teaspoon on the end of your nose without it touching your chin (or anything else)?

Very Good - 10 minutes
Super Nosy Spooner - 15 minutes

For an extra challenge try sitting down cross-legged on the floor then standing up again three times without the spoon falling off your nose. If you can do this then you are a SUPERLATIVE NOSY SPOONER.

SUPER NOSY SPOONER AWARD

Flexi-Fingers

Test the dexterity of your digits with this four-finger exercise.

You will need:
  Four coins.

FLEXI-FINGERS
1.
Turn the palm of one or your hands face upwards.

2.
Place a coin on the tip of each of your four fingers.

3.
Now try and manoeuvre them all into a pile on the tip of your first finger. You can use your thumb to help you but nothing else must touch the coins.

How quickly can you do this without dropping a coin?

Very Good - 15 seconds
Flexi-fingers - 10 seconds or less

Now here is the ticklish bit: see how quickly you can do it without using your thumb...

Very good - 15 seconds
Super Flexi-fingers
- 10 seconds or less

Super Sucker

How quickly can you suck up a glass of fizzy drink?

You will need:
   A cupful of drink.
   A glass.
   A drinking straw.

SUPER SUCKER

Pour the fizzy drink into the glass then see how quickly you can suck it up through the straw.

Very good - 10 seconds
Super Sucker - 7 seconds

The exact time you take depends on the diameter of the straw you use.

You can play a trick on someone by secretly making a small hole in their straw with a pin. As long as the hole is above the level of your victim's drink, they will not be able to suck anything up.

Circle Squashers

See if you and your friends can become Circle Squashers Supreme.

You will need:
A circle marked on the ground, 60 cm diameter.

CIRCLE SQUASHERS

1.
See how many people you can fit into your circle.

2.
Climb on top of each other and hang over the circle but do not let any part of your bodies touch the ground outside the circle.

How many circle squashers fitted into your circle for ten seconds?

Very Good - 9 people.
Circle Squashers Supreme - 11 or more people

A record number of 32 students piled on top and hung from a pillar box with an oval top of area 0.55 m sq. (Equivalent to a circle of 80 cm diameter.)

60 cm

Quick Wits

Challenge a friend to a Quick Wits Contest and see who is the quickest witted.

1.
Point to part of your friend's body and say another part. For example point to their shoulder and say "toe".

2.
Your opponent then points to a part of your body and says another part, then it's your turn again and so on...

3.
Continue this as fast as you can without the same part being mentioned or pointed to twice.

Whoever makes a mistake or pauses for more than three seconds first, loses the contest.

The first person to win three Quick Wits Contests is the quickest witted.

Noisy Challenges

Test your whistle, pop and hoot making powers with these noisy challenges.

1. WIZARD WHISTLER

1.
Take a deep breath, pucker your lips and whistle a tune. If you do not know a tune you can invent your own.

2.
For how long can you whistle tunes non-stop?

Very Good - 5 minutes
Wizard Whistler - 10 minutes or more

A Canadian stood at the Washington Monument, Washington, USA and whistled for a record 35 hours non-stop.

Try whistling when you breathe in as well as when you breathe out.

2. SUPERSONIC WHISTLER

1.
To make a really loud supersonic whistle, stick two fingers of each hand into the corners of your mouth so they fold back the tip of your tongue.

2.
Now pucker your lips and blow as hard as you can. Alter your fingers and tongue slightly until you get a super-duper sonic whistle.

3. CHEEKY POPPER

1.
Make your lips into a small, tight circle.

2.
Put a finger of your right hand into your mouth behind your left cheek.

3.
Smartly curl the finger so it snaps out of your mouth with a "pop".

4.
Now try popping with a finger of your left hand in your right cheek.

5.
By altering your mouth slightly you can change the sound of the pop. Really Cheeky Poppers can make a series of rapid pops and imitate the sound of water being poured out of a bottle.

4. EERIE OWL HOOTER

1.
Put your palms and thumbs together and clasp your fingers round the backs of your hands. Bend your thumbs and make a hollow between your palms.

2.
With your lips round the knuckles of your thumbs blow between them and make an Eerie Owl Hoot. You may have to slightly alter the position of your lips and hands.

3.
If you put a blade of grass or leaf between your thumbs you can make an ear-splitting shriek instead!

9

Giant Sunflower

How tall a sunflower can you grow?

You will need:
Some sunflower seeds.
A patch of ground to
plant them in, preferably
in a sheltered, sunny
position.

GIANT SUNFLOWER

1.
In early spring plant your
seeds 13 mm deep and water
them.

2.
The seedlings should appear
after about 14 days. Water
regularly, as necessary. The
plants will reach their full
height in mid to late summer.

What was the height of your
tallest sunflower? Get an adult
to help you measure it.

Very Good - 2 metres
Giant Sunflower - 2.5 metres

The tallest sunflower on record
is 7.76 metres.

There are many special
techniques used for growing
really giant plants and
vegetables such as, beginning
the seedlings in a greenhouse
and planting out later,
protecting them with polythene
sheets, preparing the soil well
and using suitable fertilisers.

Speedy Seedster

See how speedily you can grow a seedling from a seed.

You will need:
Seeds from a fast-growing plant such as mustard, cress or alfalfa etc.
A container with a cover.
Tissue paper.
Water.
A ruler.

SPEEDY SEEDSTER

1.
Cover the bottom of the container with several layers of the tissue paper then moisten it with water.

2.
Sprinkle some seeds onto the moistened paper.

3.
Cover the container and leave it in a warmish place and note down the time and day.

4.
Check your seeds occasionally to make sure the paper does not dry out. You will see the roots appear first, followed by the baby leaves on the stems.

How long does your speediest seedling take to grow 35 mm tall?

Very Good - 55 hours
Speedy Seedster - 48 hours or less

The world's fastest growing plant is bamboo, some species achieving rates of 91 cm per day and reaching heights of 30 metres in less than three months.

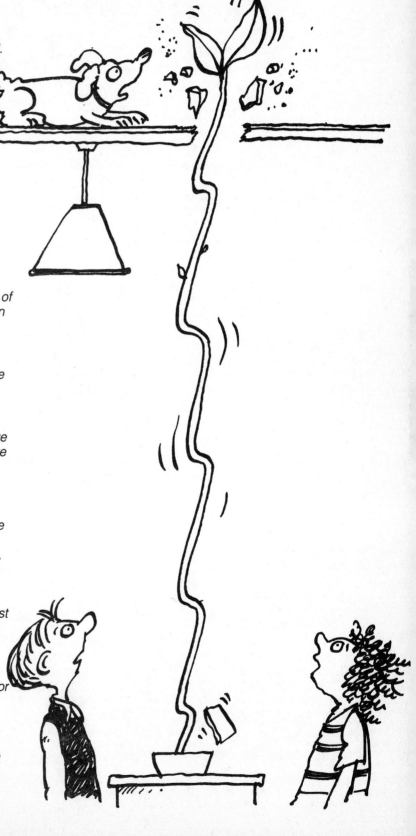

Turbo Tapper

Shuffle into the Super Challenge tap routine and stamp your mark as a Turbo Tapper.

First practise swinging your right foot forwards and backwards. On every swing just catch the ball of your foot on the ground so that it makes a 'tap'. Each forward and backward swing together, makes a 'tap tap' sound and is called a shuffle.

Do the same thing with your left foot.

NOW HAVE A GO AT THE SUPER CHALLENGE TAP ROUTINE

1.
Shuffle your right foot, 'tap tap'. Then stamp your right toe on the ground a little in front of you then your left toe on the ground a little behind you, 'stamp stamp'.

2.
Now with a little bounce put your weight on your right foot and shuffle your left foot, ' tap tap'. Then stamp your left toe on the ground a little in front of you and your right toe on the ground a little behind you, ' stamp stamp'.

3.
Then put the weight on your left foot and shuffle your right foot, ' tap tap' and so on ...

4.
Carry on doing this, ' tap tap, stamp stamp, tap tap, stamp stamp ...' routine slowly at first then gradually speed it up.

5.
Keep the swings short and the stamps light. Try and get a rhythm going so that you feel you are dancing.
You can swing your right arm as your left leg swings and your left arm as your right arm swings.

How fast can you do the Super Challenge Tap Routine?
(Each 'tap tap, stamp stamp' counts as four taps.)

Very Good - 100 taps in 30 seconds
Turbo Tapper - 140 taps in 30 seconds

The world record holder achieved speeds of 1920 taps per minute (32 per second) Another top tapper did a million taps in 23 hours 44 minutes, an average of 11.7 per second.

Nimble Knotter

If you have a knack for one-handed knotting you will soon be a renowned Nimble Knotter.

You will need:
A piece of soft string about 70 cm long.

NIMBLE KNOTTER

1.
First practise tying a knot in the string with one hand. The string should not touch anything except your hand.

2.
How many knots can you tie in the string in one minute? Try and make each knot separate so they are spread out along the string.

Very Good - 3 knots
Nimble Knotter - 5 knots

Now have a go at tying the two ends of the string together with one hand.

13

Colonel Bogey

Drink to the health of Colonel Bogey without becoming befuddled and you'll be Colonel Bogey's Buddy for life.

You will need:
A plastic cup (or use an imaginary one).

Start off sitting at a table. Read the following instructions carefully then do them as fast as you can.

1.
Stand up, raise your glass shoulder high and say, "I drink to the health of Colonel Bogey for the FIRST time".

2.
Take a short drink, sit down and put the glass on the table with ONE clear tap. Wipe your imaginary moustache ONCE with your right hand then ONCE with your left.

3.
Tap on the table ONCE with your right hand then ONCE with your left. Then tap under the table ONCE with your right hand then ONCE with your left.

4.
Stamp on the floor ONCE with your right foot then ONCE with your left. Finally rise ONCE a little way then sit down again.

Now drink to his health for the SECOND time doing everything TWICE where it says ONCE. Then for the THIRD time doing everything THREE times ... and so on.

How quickly can you drink to the health of Colonel Bogey six times?

*Very Good - 80 seconds
Colonel Bogey's Buddy For Life - 60 seconds*

Tornado Talker

Take this tongue-tying talking test and become a Tornado Talker.

TORNADO TALKER TEST

As quickly as you can, read the following words out loud, without making a mistake.

"This is the Super-Challenge Tornado Talker Test which will find out how fast you can talk. Say every word clearly without a stumble, trip, tremor or twitter. Do not dally, dither, chatter or quiver but talk quickly and try not to run out of breath."

Very Fast - 10 seconds
Tornado Talker - 5 seconds or less

Try a tornado talking race with your friends. Read a piece from a newspaper or book and see who finishes first.

Most people talk at between 70 and 180 words a minute. Much slower or faster than this and it can become difficult to understand. Some people though can speak very quickly and still be understood. The world record is 545 words in 55.8 seconds or 586 words a minute.

A1 Acrobat

Find out if you are an A1 Acrobat with the next four challenges.

THE TWIST

1.
Jump up in the air and round at the same time. Try and turn completely round so you end up facing the same way you started.

2.
If you can do this try jumping up and twisting one and a half times round so you end up facing the opposite way to the one you started from.

You will have to jump high in the air to do this.

THE SPRING

1.
Start off kneeling on the floor with your arms outstretched.

2.
Summon all your energy and leap up to a standing position.

3.
Now kneel down again and leap up again as before.

Try and do this five times in a row.

JUMPING JACK

1.
Start off squatting on the floor with your arms folded.

2.
Now spring up into the air onto your heels and throw your arms out wide. Then immediately drop back to the starting position.

Try and do this five times in 15 seconds.

THE LIFT

1.
Sit on the floor with your legs bent in front of you.

2.
Put your palms down flat on the floor either side of you.

3.
Now lift your body up so only your hands are touching the floor.

4.
Practise this lift until you can do it for five seconds or more.

When you have successfully done all four challenges you are definitely an *A1 ACROBAT*.

17

Super Snail

You won't get very far with these next three slothful challenges.

TORTOISE TALKER

How slowly can you read out loud the following words without pausing except for breath.

"It is harder to speak slowly than fast so you must really stretch out each sound to make it last."

Very Good - 45 seconds
Tortoise Talker - 60 seconds

SNAIL-PACED PEDALLER

How slowly can you ride your bike without falling off?

1.
Mark two lines on the ground, three metres apart.

2.
Ride your bike up to the first line and start timing as your front wheel crosses it.

3.
Cycle as slowly as you can in a straight line until your front wheel crosses the other line.

How long did you take without putting a foot down?

Very Good - 5 seconds
Snail-paced Pedaller - 10 seconds or more

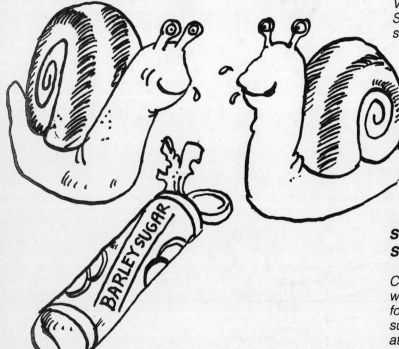

SUPER SLUGGISH SUCKER

Challenge a friend to see which of you can suck a sweet for the longest. Both start sucking the same sort of sweet at the same time.

Whoever is the last to have any sweet left is the Super Sluggish Sucker.

Pea Pusher

Propel a pea along the floor
with your nose and win the
Pea Pusher Prize.

You will need:
A pea (fresh or dried).

PRIZE PEA PUSHER

1.
Mark out a distance of two
metres on the floor.

2.
Put the pea at the start and
push it along the floor just
using your nose until you
reach the finish. The pea must
stay in contact with your nose
all the time.

How quickly did you reach the
end?

Very Good - 75 seconds
Prize Pea Pusher - 60 seconds
or less

You can also have pea pusher
races with your friends and
see who finishes first.

Tiddly Winker

How quickly can you pot ten winks?

You will need:
Eleven plastic counters (known as winks).
You can use large buttons instead.
A saucer.

TIDDLY WINKER

1.
Practise tiddling your winks by holding one in your hand and pressing it down onto the edge of one lying on the ground until it shoots into the air. See if you can pot the wink into the saucer.

2.
Start off with a wink 45 cm away from the saucer, then, tiddling it as many times as necessary, pot it into the saucer.

How quickly can you pot ten winks into the saucer from a distance of 45 cm? All ten winks must end up in the saucer.

*Very Good - 60 seconds
Tiddly Winker - 45 seconds.*

The record for potting winks from a distance of 45 cm is twenty-four in 21.8 seconds.

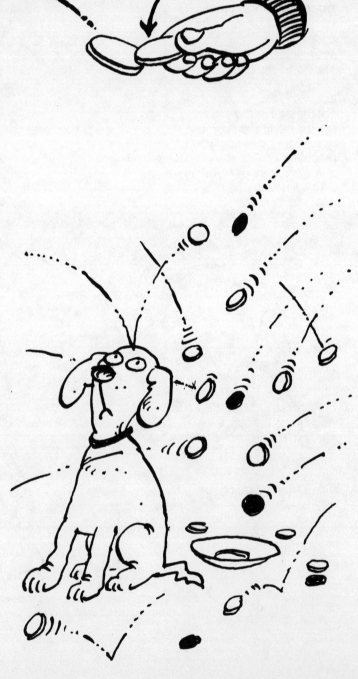

Pyramid Puzzler

This puzzle could boggle your brains for quite a while before you manage to solve it.

You will need:
Five coins of different sizes.

PYRAMID PUZZLER

1.
Imagine that there are three positions; A, B and C. Pile the coins into a pyramid at position A.

2.
The aim is to move one coin at a time from one pile to another and end up with the coins in a pyramid at position B. To do this you will have to use position C.

3.
Only move coins from the top of a pile and do not put larger coins on top of smaller ones.

How quickly can you move the pyramid from A to B?

Very Good - 3 minutes
Power Puzzler - 2 minutes

The least number of moves required to move the pyramid from A to B is 31. If you manage to do it in this number of moves then you are a PERFECT PYRAMID PUZZLER.

String Spinner

A little striving at spinning a piece of string will turn you into a Skilful String Spinner.

You will need:
A piece of string about 120 cm long.
A soft weight such as a sponge or a rag tied into a ball.

STRING SPINNER

1.
Tie the sponge to one end of the string. Wrap the other end a few times around your fingers.

2.
Start off with the sponge to one side and the string taut behind your legs.

3.
Swing the string so that the sponge moves in a wide arc a little above the ground.

4.
As the string swings round in front of your legs, jump over it. You will have to bend down and hold the string near the ground to do this. Continue swinging the string and jump over it when it comes round again and so on ...

How many times in a row can you jump over the string?

Very Good - 20 times
Super String Spinner - 50 or more

MORE STRING SPINNING STUNTS

1. HOP SPINNER

How many times in a row can you spin the string as before but this time hop over it on one foot?

Very Good - 20 times
Hot-rod Hop Spinner - 50 or more times

2. HANDS FEET FLYER

Support yourself with one hand and two feet on the ground. Spin the string with the other hand so you quickly have to lift your hand over it first then your feet. Continue spinning the string and see how many times in a row you can do this. Try and keep the sponge off the ground as much as you can.

Very Good - 15 times
Hands Feet Flyer - 30 or more times

3. TOP TEAM SPINNERS

You will need:
A length of rope or heavy string 3 metres long
A cloth tied into a ball.

Tie the cloth ball onto the end of the string. Hold the other end of the string then get your friends to stand in a circle around you. Now spin the rope round and see how many of them can jump over it at the same time for five spins.

Very Good - 6 friends
Top Team Spinners - 8 or more

Carry on spinning and eliminate anyone that makes a mistake. See who can stay in the longest.

Neck Knot

Try not to get too knotted up over this crazy challenge.

NECK KNOT

1.
Clasp the fingers of both hands together in front of you.

2.
Slip one elbow over the bend of the other so your arms cross over. Keep your hands clasped together all the time.

3.
Now move your arms apart and pass them right over your head until your clasped hands touch the back of your neck.

4.
Practise the neck knot a few times and see how quickly you can do it.

Here is a further challenge to try when you have mastered the neck knot. Tie a neck knot then sit cross-legged on the floor and stand up again without your knees touching the ground or using anything for support.

24

Prime Puffer

Have you enough puff to become a Prime Puffer?

You will need:
  A ping pong ball.
  A drinking straw.

PRIME PUFFER

1.
Hold the straw upright and gently blow through it.

2.
Carefully place the ping pong ball so that it floats just above the end of the straw.

3.
Just as you begin to run out of breath, blow the ball a little higher in the air, take a quick, deep breath then blow out again and catch the ball in the air stream.

For how long can you keep the ping pong ball floating in the air?

Very Good - 3 seconds
Prime Puffer - 6 seconds or more

For an extra challenge try keeping two balls up in the air at the same time. If you can do this for 5 seconds you are a PRIME PUFFER.

Heel Flicker

The Slick Heel Flicker title is yours for the taking if you accomplish this heel flicking feat.

You will need:
Ten balls of paper.
A waste-paper-basket or similar container.

HEEL FLICKER

1.
Put the balls on the floor about one metre from the basket.

2.
With your back to the basket, grip one of the balls between your heels.

3.
Now jump up in the air with both feet together and try and flick the ball backwards into the basket. When the first ball is in the basket do the same with another one and so on ...

How many "flicks" do you need to get all the balls into the basket?

Very Good - 11 or 12
Slick Heel Flicker - 10

How quickly can you flick all ten balls into the basket?

Very Good - 60 seconds
Even Slicker Heel Flicker
- 30 seconds

Quintuple Catcher

Win acclaim as a Champion Quintuple Catcher with this tricky stunt.

DO THIS CHALLENGE OUT OF DOORS.

You will need:
A plastic cup.
Five marbles.

QUINTUPLE CATCHER

1.
Hold the empty cup in one hand and the five marbles in the other.

2.
Throw a marble up into the air, at least two metres above your head and catch it in the cup without it jumping out again.

3.
Leave the first marble in the cup and throw up a second marble. Catch this one in the cup without either jumping out. Then do the same with the next marble and so on ...

How many throws do you need to get all five marbles in the cup?

Very Good - 6, 7 or 8 throws
Champion Quintuple
Catcher - 5 throws

It will help stop the marbles jumping out if you move the cup downwards just as you catch each one.

Micro Maestro

Tackle these microscopic challenges, collect three Micro Merits and you will be a Micro Maestro.

You will need:
Some uncooked rice (large-grained rice is easiest).
Two cocktail sticks.
A thimble.
A saucer (for Tiddly Rice).

THIMBLE FILL

1.
Stand the thimble with its open end upwards.

2.
Put a small pile of rice near the thimble.

3.
Hold the two cocktail sticks in one hand as if they were chopsticks. Hold one stick between your thumb and first finger and the other with your first and second finger on one side and third on the other. The tip of your little finger controls this stick.

4.
Carefully pick up a single grain of rice between the ends of the sticks and put it into the thimble. Then do the same with another grain and so on ...

How quickly can you fill the thimble in this way?

Very Good - 5 minutes
Micro Merit - 4 minutes

RICE RACE

Start with a small pile of rice on the table. Now using a cocktail stick in each hand, push the rice along the table and form a single line with each grain touching the next.

How quickly can you form a line 30 cm long?

Very Good - 2 minutes
Micro Merit - 1 minute 30 seconds

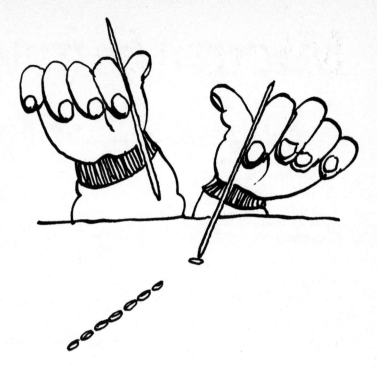

TIDDLY RICE

1.
Put the saucer on a smooth table with a pile of rice near it.

2.
Now press down on one end of a grain of rice with a cocktail stick and shoot the grain into the saucer.

Practise this a few times and you will get better at it.

How many grains of rice can you shoot into the saucer in ten minutes? (The rice must stay in the saucer to count.)

Very Good - 5 grains
Micro Merit - 10 grains

When you have three Micro Merits you are a MICRO MAESTRO.

29

Soccer Supremo

Find out how fine a footballer you are with the Soccer Supremo Challenge.

You will need:
 A soccerball or beachball.

FIRST PRACTISE THESE TRAINING EXERCISES.

1.
Balance the ball on your right foot while the foot is raised a little off the ground. Count slowly to ten.

Then do the same thing using your other foot.

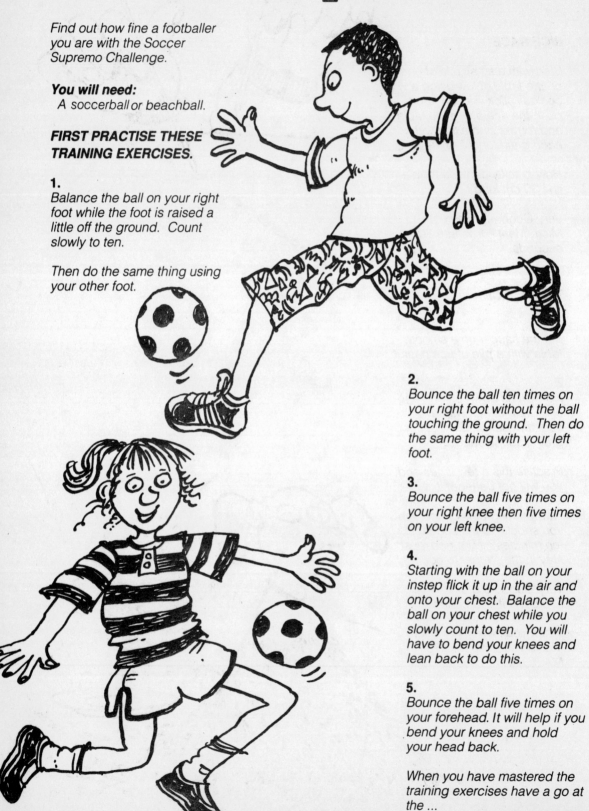

2.
Bounce the ball ten times on your right foot without the ball touching the ground. Then do the same thing with your left foot.

3.
Bounce the ball five times on your right knee then five times on your left knee.

4.
Starting with the ball on your instep flick it up in the air and onto your chest. Balance the ball on your chest while you slowly count to ten. You will have to bend your knees and lean back to do this.

5.
Bounce the ball five times on your forehead. It will help if you bend your knees and hold your head back.

When you have mastered the training exercises have a go at the ...

SOCCER SUPREMO CHALLENGE

1.
Start off with the ball balanced on your right foot then flick it up into the air and onto your forehead.

2.
Balance or bounce the ball on your forehead then catch it on your chest.

3.
Next let if roll down to your knee, flick it from one knee to the other then catch it on your left foot.

4.
Lastly flick it to your right foot then up in the air and onto your forehead again and so on ...

How many times can you do this routine without handling or dropping the ball?

Very Good - 2 times
Soccer Supremo - 3 times or more

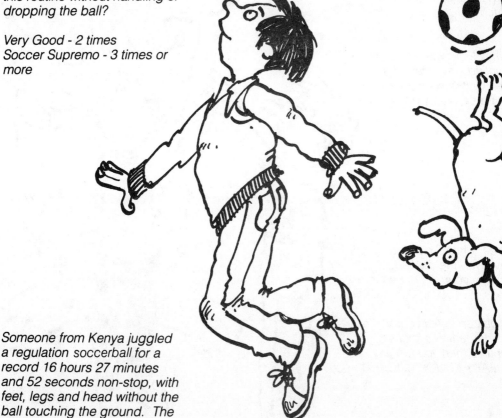

Someone from Kenya juggled a regulation soccerball for a record 16 hours 27 minutes and 52 seconds non-stop, with feet, legs and head without the ball touching the ground. The same person also headed a soccerball non-stop for five hours.

Major Look (Made You Look)

Your victim will have to keep on guard to repel this sneaky challenge.

MAJOR LOOK

1.
Bet a friend that you can make them look three times.

2.
For example: suddenly point out of the window and ask "What's that?" or you can invent things such as: "Look at that enormous spider!" or "Have you seen my new watch?"

3.
If they look where you are pointing, say "Major Look!" then wait until they are off guard before trying again.

4.
Three "Major Looks" and you have won the challenge. Of course, your victim can try to make you look three times first.

If you can make your victim look three times in fifteen minutes then you are a SNEAKY MAJOR LOOKER.

Dodgy Doodles

Discover your doodling dexterity with these two testing challenges.

You will need:
Paper and a pencil.

GYRO-DOODLER

1.
Sit at a table, lift one foot off the ground and make circular movements with it. Try to write on the paper at the same time. Write your name or copy something from a book.

2.
Continue writing and change the direction of your foot movement. Now have a go at writing while gyrating your other foot.

With practice and concentration you will be able to write normally while either foot gyrates and become a DAB-HANDED GYRO-DOODLER.

FOOT DOODLER

1.
Take off one of your shoes and socks and stick the pencil, pointing downwards, between two of your toes. Now gripping the pencil with your toes write your name on the paper. You can try writing with the pencil between different toes.

2.
At first the writing will be big and scrawly but with effort you will get it smaller and neater. If you can write your first and last names in a space of less than 10 cm you are a FLEXI-TOED FOOT DOODLER.

For an extra challenge try and pick up the pencil and put it between your toes without using your hands – use both your bare feet this time. Have a go at writing whole sentences and drawing with your feet.

Card Toppler

Can you topple a whole pack of cards in one go and become a Tip-Top Toppler.

You will need:
A pack of playing cards.

CARD TOPPLER

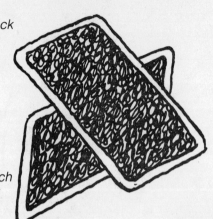

1.
Lean two cards against each other so that one is upright and the other on its side.

2.
Do the same for a second pair of cards, putting them about a card's width from the first pair and so on until all the cards are standing in pairs in a straight line, facing the same way.

3.
Now push over the end card lying on its side so that the first pair topples over and knocks the second pair over and so on ....

How many cards toppled over with one push?

Very Good - 30 cards
Tip-Top Toppler - All 52 cards

If any of your cards do not topple over, adjust the angle between the cards and the distance between the pairs.

NOW TRY YOUR HAND AT THESE OTHER CARD TOPPLING STUNTS.

1. DIAGONAL TOPPLE

Set up the cards in pairs as before but with each upright card to one side and each pair moved over half-a-card's width.

Your cards will now topple over in a diagonal line.

2. HERRINGBONE

This time the pairs of cards face outwards at an angle alternatively to the right then to the left. You will have to experiment to get the best angles.

Your toppling cards will now form a herringbone pattern.

3. FAN

It is easy to get the first pair of cards to knock over two pairs which in turn knock over three pairs and so on .... You will then have a toppling fan of cards.

4. ALL CHANGE

To get a line of toppling cards to change direction have the pair on the end positioned between the two lines. Set up this pair so that when the card on its side falls, the upright card topples over it and sets off the next line. The card on its side should be less upright than normal and the upright card more so.

You can also try to get a line of toppling cards to knock over a house of cards. For spectacular card toppling effects you can use more than one pack of cards.

Coin Balancer

Try balancing coins on the back of your hand and become a Bumper Balancer.

You will need:
Some coins.

COIN BALANCE

1.
Start off with one of your hands in front of you, unsupported and palm downwards.
Now with the other hand build a single pile of coins on the back of your first hand.

2.
When you have enough coins in the pile carefully move your hand with the coins on the back until your arm is fully outstretched and at shoulder height.

How many coins can you hold out like this for ten seconds?

Very Good - 30 coins
Bumper Balancer - 35 or more coins

Now in the same way see how long you can hold out a pile of at least twenty coins.

Very Good - 45 seconds
Brilliant Balancer - 75 seconds

For an extra challenge, out-of-doors, see how long you can balance a paper or plastic cup, half filled with water, on the back of your hand, with arm outstretched. It is said to be impossible for anyone to do this for more than seven minutes.

First-Rate Rotator

Rapid gyrations could turn you into a First-Rate Rotator.

You will need:
  A jam jar.
  A small ball.

FIRST-RATE ROTATOR

1.
Put the ball on a smooth surface and place the jam jar over it.

2.
Now move the jam jar in small, rapid circles so that the ball rolls around the inside of the jar. You will find it best to do this with one hand.

3.
When the ball is spinning fast enough you will be able to lift the jar clear of the table without the ball falling out.

Keep the ball rolling round inside the jar and see how long you can hold the jar up without the ball falling out.

Very Good - 15 seconds
First-Rate Rotator - 30 seconds

Centrifugal force keeps the rolling ball on the side of the jar, the same force that prevents the earth from crashing into the sun.

Jumbo Juggler

Try your hand at juggling and work your way up to a Jumbo Talented Juggler.

JUMBO ONER

You will need:
One ball.

Throw the ball from one hand to the other and back again. Keep your hands about waist height and throw the ball a little higher than your head.

How many times can you do this without dropping the ball?

Very Good - 50 times
Jumbo Oner - 100 or more

JUMBO TWOER

You will need:
Two balls.

1.
Start off with a ball in each hand and do a Jumbo Oner with both balls at the same time.

2.
Throw up one ball first and as it reaches its highest point throw up the second ball so it passes just below the first one.

3.
Catch the first ball and quickly throw it up again. Catch the second ball and throw it up as the first one reaches its highest point and so on ...

4.
Keep throwing the balls up high and make inward scooping movements with your hands as they catch and throw the balls with one movement. With practise you will get a rhythm going.

How long can you Jumbo Twoer without dropping a ball?

Very Good - 15 seconds
Jumber Twoer - 30 seconds

When you are a well-practised Jumbo Twoer you can have a go at the Tricky Jumbo Three-er.

JUMBO THREE-ER

You will need:
Three balls.

1.
Start off with two balls in one hand and one in the other and do a Jumbo Twoer and Oner at the same time.

2.
First throw up one of the two balls, then the single ball, followed by the third ball. Each time one ball peaks, throw up the next and so on ...

If you can Jumbo Three-er for 15 seconds then you certainly are a JUMBO TALENTED JUGGLER.

Finger Knitter

You will need fumble-free
fingers to finish the Natty
Finger Knitter Challenge.

You will need:
 A piece of soft string or
 wool 1 metre long.

FINGER KNITTER

1.
Fold the string in half and put
your thumb in the loop.

2.
Bend your first finger over the
top string and under the lower
string so it passes round the
back of the finger.

3.
Repeat for each finger in turn.

4.
After your little finger let the
string ends lie across your
palm and continue knitting
back along your fingers.

5.
Now slip the loop off your little
finger and pull the ends of the
string. If you have done your
knitting correctly the string
should slide off the other
fingers.

How fast can you finger knit
just using one hand and pull
the string off?

Very Good - 15 seconds
Natty Finger Knitter
- 10 seconds

For an extra difficult challenge
try finger knitting both hands
with a double length piece of
string.

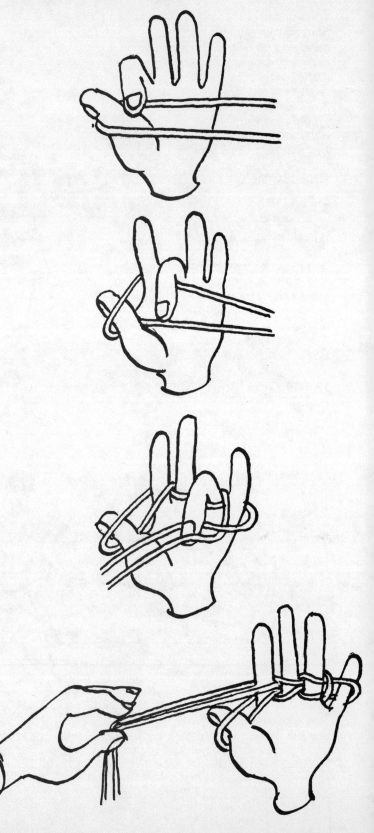

Perfect Pourer

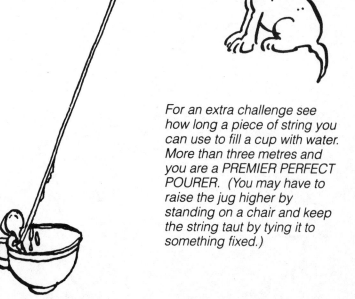

Get water flowing down a piece of string and you will make a splash as a Perfect Pourer.

It is best to try this challenge out-of-doors.

You will need:
A jug.
A cup.
A piece of string 1 metre long.
A teaspoon.
Water.

PERFECT POURER

1.
Tie one end of the string to the jug handle and the other end to the teaspoon.

2.
Fill the jug with water. Put the cup on the ground with the teaspoon inside it.

3.
Raise the jug of water. Make sure the string stays taut and passes across the spout. Now carefully pour the water down the string. You may have to raise or lower the jug to do this.

If you can fill the cup by pouring a jugful of water down the string you are a PERFECT POURER.

Water molecules tend to cling to surfaces which is why the water stays on the string.

For an extra challenge see how long a piece of string you can use to fill a cup with water. More than three metres and you are a PREMIER PERFECT POURER. (You may have to raise the jug higher by standing on a chair and keep the string taut by tying it to something fixed.)

Crazy Olympics

Challenge your friends to a Crazy Olympic Pentathlon and see who wins the gold medal.

HOP, SKIP AND JUMP

1.
First mark a line on the ground.

2.
Competitors take turns to stand behind the line and hold their right ankle with their right hand and their left ankle with their left hand. Then do a hop, skip and a jump and see how far you can get.

3.
Everyone has three goes and marks their best effort. The competitor who covers the greatest distance from the line wins.

FOOT PUTT

You will need:
A ball (or a wet sponge).

1.
Competitors take turns to lie on their backs and pick up and throw the ball with their bare feet. Handling the ball is not allowed.

2.
Everyone in turn foot putts from the same position and where the ball first lands is marked.

After three rounds the contestant with the longest putt wins.

HIGH JUMP

You will need:
 A cane.
 Two pieces of wood (or books) for support.

1.
Raise the cane a few inches off the ground and support it each end with the wood.

2.
Competitors take turns to try and jump over the cane, keeping both feet together.

3.
After every round raise the cane slightly and see who can jump the highest.

STOMACH SPRINT

This is best done on grass or a soft mat.

1.
First mark two lines three metres apart.

2.
Competitors lie on their stomachs behind the first line, right hand grasping right ankle, left hand grasping left ankle.

3.
On the word 'Go' everyone slithers on their stomachs as fast as they can without letting go of their ankles. The first person across the finishing line wins.

BARMY BALANCE

1.
Contestants start off kneeling on the floor holding their left ankle with their left hand.

2.
On the word 'Go' everyone lifts their left leg clear of the ground and sees who can balance like this for the longest.

The person that wins the most events is the CRAZY OLYMPIC PENTATHLON GOLD MEDALLIST.

Super Spiraller

Make this spiral out of cocktail sticks and you will be a First-Rate Super Spiraller.

You will need:
160 cocktail sticks, or headless matches (sold in model shops)

SUPER SPIRALLER

1.
Make a square out of four of the sticks so that two of them lie on top of the other two.

2.
Make another square out of four more sticks on top of the first square but rotated slightly.

3.
Continue adding four more sticks at a time, rotating each square a little bit more in the same direction. You should use about forty sticks to build a spiral with a quarter turn in it.

4.
Build your spiral as neatly as you can without it leaning over. It will look better if all the sticks lie one above another.

How high a spiral can you build?

Very Good - Half turn spiral (using 80 sticks)
Super Spiraller - Full turn spiral (using 160 sticks)

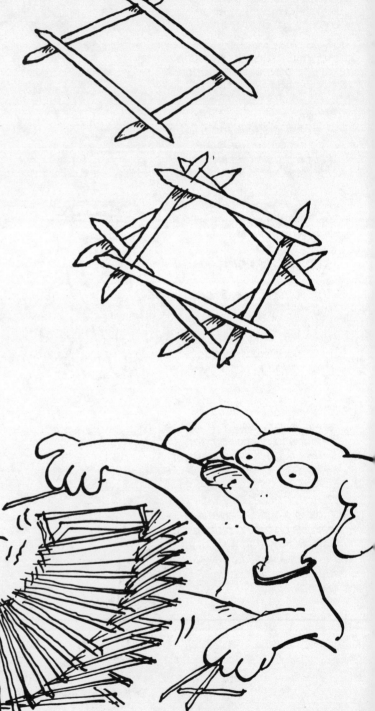

Master Match Builder

If you can build this arch of matches you are a Master Match Builder.

USE HEADLESS MATCHES AS SOLD IN MODEL SHOPS FOR THIS CHALLENGE.

You will need:
  Twenty-one headless matches or cocktail sticks.

MASTER MATCH BUILDER

1.
Start off with nine matches and build the top of the arch.

2.
You may find it easier to first lay the five horizontal matches in position then gently raise one of the end matches and slide in two of the legs. Do the same for the other side.

3.
Now carefully add another horizontal match and two legs to each side of your arch. When you have done this and built an arch of fifteen matches you are a VERY GOOD MATCH BUILDER

4.
If you can add a further horizontal match and two legs to each side and make an arch of twenty-one matches, then you are a MASTER MATCH BUILDER.

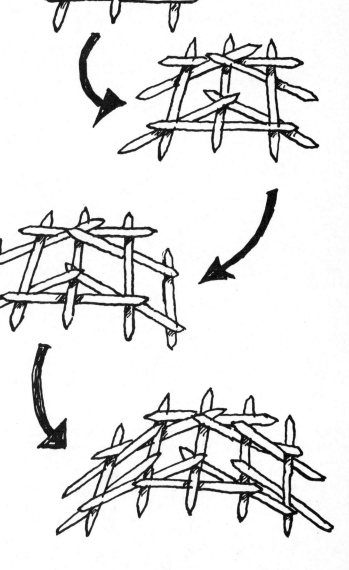

One Man Band

Can you play five musical instruments all at the same time and become a Super One Man Bander?

You can make your own musical instruments. Here are five easy ones to make:

1. GUITAR

An open box or other container with three or four rubber bands stretched over it.

Twang the rubber bands and adjust them by pulling them tighter or looser.

2. DRUM

A wooden stick or ruler fixed to your foot with rubber bands and a flat piece of tin or wood.

3. MARACA

A small container and lid with some rice or beads in it fixed to your foot with rubber bands.

4. CYMBAL

An up-side-down cup with a saucepan lid on top of it and a wooden stick.

5. GAZOO

A cardboard tube from a roll of kitchen paper or similar.

After you have made your instruments, practise playing them all at the same time.

1.
Make humming noises down your gazoo.

2.
Tap the edge of the saucepan lid to make cymbal noises.

3.
Bang your drum, shake your maraca and twang your guitar.

When you can play a tune using all five instruments then you are a SUPER ONE MAN BANDER.

You can make more instruments and try and play them at the same time.

Now beat that ...

... The world record one-man band uses 108 musical instruments.

AN ANGUS & ROBERTSON BOOK
An imprint of HarperCollinsPublishers

First published in Australia in 1992 by
CollinsAngus&Robertson Publishers Pty Limited (ACN 009 913 517)
A division of HarperCollinsPublishers (Australia) Pty Limited
25–31 Ryde Road, Pymble, NSW 2073, Australia
First published in the United Kingdom in 1991 by
HarperCollinsPublishers Limited
77– 85 Fulham Palace Road, London W6 8JB, United Kingdom
HarperCollinsPublishers (New Zealand) Limited
31 View Road, Glenfield, Auckland 10, New Zealand

National Library of Australia
Cataloguing-in-Publication data:
Dinneen, John.
   Superchallenge 2.
   ISBN 0 207 17373 7.
   1. Indoor games - Juvenile literature. 2. Puzzles - Juvenile
   literature. I. Title. II. Title: Superchallenge two.
793.7

Printed in Australia by Griffin Press
 5 4 3 2 1
96 95 94 93 92